A catalogue record for this book is available from the British Library.

First edition 2018
Published by NR Publishing

Cover photograph by Kat Smith
Other image by Bruce Mars
(Source: www.pexels.com)

For recordings and other publications by Nick Roach Teachings, please visit the website: www.nickroach.uk.

© **2018 Nick Roach Teachings**
www.nickroach.uk

The

Secret Life

of

Emotion

God's Emotional

~~Nightmare~~ ~~Ordeal~~ ~~Dream~~

World

Nick Roach

How This Book Came to Be

In 2005, having reached a point at which I felt it appropriate to begin teaching, and having set up the website the year before, we published our first book, *Enlightenment, the Simple Path: Answering questions such as 'Who am I?' and 'What's it all about?'*. A year later we removed a lot of the material from the website, and along with some new articles put this into the second book, *Essays in Truth – Glimpses into Reality.*

There was then a gap of ten years during which I continued to teach through the website, responding to emails and meeting people for one-to-ones, and later we got on to Facebook, and this also became a major means by which we communicated with people.

Finally, the circumstances of life changed and I was able to devote some time to publishing my spiritual autobiography, writing up the notes of the last twenty or so years since I began following what is known as The Spiritual Path, during which every insight and experience had been recorded in detail. This was entitled *A Dream It May Be, but the Dream Goes On!* (from an insight that had made a huge impression on me in my early twenties). And as I read and re-read my own story a number of times during the creation of the book, the underlying theme that stood out for me was partly the role emotion played in my journey, but perhaps more importantly, the deepening of my understanding of the emotion's journey, and particularly its relationship with the physical environment as a whole. The latter was even amazing to me as I read it all back. And much of it also seemed to be new to everyone else, at least to the people I was in contact with (many of whom were not only spiritually experienced but some were teachers in their own right).

So the book was published, and I was convinced it was going to be a revelation to any and all who read it. Surely no-one could help but be as amazed as I was about what is uncovered and explained in some detail, and particularly when this is supported by the story of my life describing how I came to such knowledge.

However, it appears the underlying story of the emotion itself, which I thought was the most important part of the book, became lost in my own story. And while reviews and feedback from people who read the book were all positive, very rarely did they relate to the journey of the emotion.

As a result, we felt it appropriate to give it its very own book. Here I will describe the life-cycle of the emotion from the initial 'birth' to its eventual demise. But more than that, I will describe clearly how one can help the emotion along its way, ultimately taking the person out of emotional suffering and into the experience of emotional freedom known as Enlightenment or Self Realisation, leading to Liberation. But even more than that, we will understand the role emotion plays in the creation and development of the physical environment, and specifically, in the circumstances of one's life. And how one can use this knowledge to improve the life experience – not to get what one wants so much as how to quickly learn the lessons that a specific difficult situation demands so that one can move on, and life can become a pleasure.

You will notice throughout the book I refer to the individual as 'He' or 'Him', etc. (and later 'he' or 'him'). This begins as a reference to the traditional perspective of God, and this gender allocation is continued through the book for simplicity only.

If you would like to know more about my journey and how I came to know the contents of this book (or, why I claim to know what's in this book, if it seems too outrageous to believe), please read my autobiography.

In the meantime I hope you enjoy what follows.

Nick Roach

Contents

The Myth
(Part 1)

Ask most people what emotion is and they're likely to reply with a simple description along the lines of, "It's what you feel when you're unhappy or angry about something", though this may quickly be followed with the addition of more positive feelings such as 'happiness' and 'love'.

If a therapist is asked the same question, their response is likely to include the description that emotion from every painful event or experience from birth is stored in the unconscious mind, which in the therapeutic process is often likened to a rucksack of rocks being carried for an entire life, all the time getting heavier and heavier, weighing the person down mentally, and at times eventually leading to what is termed 'mental health problems'.

Likewise, a psychologist may describe how the stored emotion as per the therapist (above) affects and indeed determines the individual's behaviour and thought patterns, having directly but silently created the person they are today, and in turn is responsible for the person they will yet become.

Ask a scientist what emotion is, and s/he is likely to reply with a detailed description of the various chemicals that are released in the brain, and more-so in which specific area, in a given situation.

And the replies can be different again when speaking with people who are regarded as spiritually aware. Those interested in what are often termed 'New Age' philosophies can tend to work with various practices towards releasing 'negative energies' (or emotions) which they also acknowledge as having accumulated, whilst seeking to promote the positive ones. And then we have more intellectual spiritual people who can dismiss emotion in all its forms as irrelevant and something that just happens, instead focusing on the essence or idea of union or oneness that spiritual teachings often hold up as the end goal.

I called this chapter 'The Myth' because as accurate as the above may be, they all describe how the emotions begin and end with the body; the emotion itself has no 'life' before or after the person lives and dies. And it has no value besides affecting one's enjoyment of living. And this is the greatest misunderstanding of emotion and one I hope to address with this book.

Genesis

"In the beginning God created the heaven and the earth. And the earth was without form, and void; and darkness was upon the face of the deep. And the Spirit of God moved upon the face of the waters. And God said, Let there be light: and there was light."

– Genesis 1:1–3

The above are the very first words of *The Holy Bible* (King James version, 2000) where God begins to create the material universe. (In case anyone's wondering, I am not religious at all, but having followed the 'spiritual life' for about twenty-five years to date, from the perspective of 'Self-development', I can see in my own knowledge and experience what many of the religious texts of different religions are referring to.) I have often used stories from both Buddhism and the *Bhagavad Gita* as well, as they can also be very helpful in pointing to the Greater Truth.

So, the above quote from the Bible SEEMS to begin at the very beginning, but that is not the case. If you look again you will notice

9

there is something that has already happened prior to the above: Why did God create heaven and earth? What was it that happened to prompt the need or action?

It is common, if not inevitable, that people interested in spiritual matters regard everything as being one. And although it's not the main focus of those who follow religions, the teachings do tend to refer to one God or omnipotent 'Being' creating everything; thus, again, everything is 'one'.

This book is entitled *The Secret Life of Emotion*, with the subheading *God's Emotional World*, because these are what I will be talking about. But these are NOT two separate subjects. They are one and the same, and once understood, this is so truly amazing and even outrageous that it's almost, or perhaps it is totally impossible to believe and more ridiculous to take seriously. But here goes:

Prior to God (or whatever name one uses for the one Being) creating 'heaven and earth', there was an impulse to do so, and THIS is the origin of what we call emotion: the wish or need to 'do' something; and this is what has been omitted from the Bible and yet it's arguably the most important aspect, as everything else stems from this.

The text goes on to describe God creating the physical environment. To us, we perceive and experience this place as a fixed, solid structure which exists independently of us and through which we walk and with which we interact. But Eastern traditions teach that this is not the case, and both Buddhism and Hinduism use the term 'maya' which means 'illusion' (referring to the appearance of separation where there is none, as everything is still 'one'). Though another description regularly used in the West by Spiritually Enlightened people is that it's [like] a 'dream': In a dream when asleep in bed, everything appears separate, and one can walk around and talk with other people, and yet it's all occurring within one's own mind, created by one's own unconscious and driven by the emotional need to experience whatever the scenario is. And it could even be said that the mind dreaming it (i.e. you) is omnipotent, as you are in fact everywhere and in everything. And although admittedly a dream when asleep is often more flexible with regards to the laws of physics (okay, sometimes there aren't any) compared with the waking world, and also the 'waking dream' continues pretty much where we left it when we wake the next day (allowing for the few hours whilst we've been in bed asleep), when viewed from a spiritual perspective this physical environment fits many of the characteristics of a dream nonetheless.

Note: Just out of interest, with regards to the above, I had the insight in my early twenties that this place is a dream, as I connected with the stillness within me, and admittedly it was terrifying at the time. But this developed and deepened over the years to become the experience of having a lucid dream in which I was/am indeed interacting with 'my' (the One) mind, and later the experience was of the dream and the Dreamer merging to become one and the same. So the dream analogy works for me.

So what we have now is God, or the one Being having the (emotional or energetic) impulse to create SOMETHING within Itself, and thus the dream of separation begins.

However, the Bible goes on to describe God as a separate independent entity, apparently leaving Adam and Eve, Man and Woman to enjoy the fruits of life that He had provided. He would visit them, speak with them, monitor and even judge them, but He was not them. And again this is a huge error in the Genesis story in the Bible. It sets the scene that God is 'up there' somewhere, an 'all-knowing' Being to be revered and feared, but never 'realised' within oneself – at least not outside of mythical stories of special people. If only the story had included the words 'God put Himself into the body of Adam, so He could see through Adam's eyes and experience the world in a body. God then made Eve so that He would have another to love and with whom He could share the experience and enjoyment of the creation He had put so much love into.' Imagine how our perspective and understanding of life, and particularly religious and spiritual teachings, would be different if that had been included? Because that is what happened!

The Dream of Separation

So God is now in a body, able to interact with His (dreamt) environment. His wish to experience more and more continued to grow with each new event, and it was amazing, but it wasn't enough. As soon as the experience he'd been wishing for materialised, he found the satisfaction ended quickly, and he looked forward to the next; and it was not long before he forgot that he was creating it all, instead focusing entirely on his own satisfaction, spending most of his time in his imagination. (You'll have noticed the loss of the capital 'H' in front of 'He' and 'His' above, as God is reduced, as far as he can tell, to playing the role of just one of the great many people who are doing their best to get by.)

So he looked forward to what he thought would make him 'happy', and remembered past experiences which in turn also stimulated nice feelings, all to distract from being conscious in the moment where there were no feelings at all.

But while each positive feeling was a 'high', a vacuum happened as a result, and he found a nice feeling would often be followed by its opposite, of being unhappy. Though he didn't really mind, as he was enjoying the turmoil, the drama, and the uncertainty of what would be and the subsequent ups and downs of the emotion.

He didn't know that if he had held on to the moment, the awareness of being now, and endured the emotion consciously without getting lost in his imagination, it would have subsided, as emotion cannot survive in the moment. It requires the attention to let go of 'now' and go into the world of thinking, and the pendulum would have stopped swaying, and he would have been free of the endless cycle. But it didn't matter. He didn't want to know.

What About Love?

Every so often, in the midst of the merry-go-round of emotion, he would meet someone with whom he felt an amazing connection. What was this? He felt complete, whole, as if he could stay with this person forever and never leave. This was incredible!

But it was not to last. As soon as the other went away, even if only for a short time, the wonderful sensation would leave also. He would think about them, remember them and imagine all about them in an attempt to reconnect with what he had lost, but nothing worked. It was so painful. What was this?

And then they would return. 'Thank God! I am complete again. Don't ever leave me!' he'd pray.

The secret that he had long since forgotten is that this is all him. And the very thing he is praying to, the almighty that he calls God, even if he doesn't really believe it exists, is himself, his true being. But suggest that to him now and he'll laugh it off as ridiculous. And more so, he has become so addicted to the emotional feelings, allowing them to determine and dictate everything he thinks, says and does, that he would never accept that this love that he finds so amazing is not actually emotion anyway. However, it's not based in a wanting, nor a looking forward or back, not when he's with the person. When it's present, it's in the moment now. This other person whom he loves so much – this dream character in his admittedly incredible dream world – is reflecting some of his own true nature, his own sense of being back to him, thus putting him, through no effort on his part, into the moment and reconnecting him with his true self that he had spent so long fleeing from. That's why he feels complete, albeit temporarily.

The above explains why love is so incredible sometimes, but does not explain why he keeps losing this wonderful experience when he's not with the other person.

He loses it because he lets go of it. He has become so accustomed to living in his imagination, chasing the feelings related to what is not here now, that when the mirror of his true nature that this person provides is not present, he does not know to feel inside, to consciously connect with his inner being and stay with that. He wouldn't know where to look anyway. So he misses the reminder of the truth within and fails to learn the lesson that is provided. This was his opportunity to begin to reconnect with the essence of all that is: Himself, God.

So as time passes, the strength of the incredible sense of being complete becomes buried once again under the mass of emotion and thinking, and it's gone.

Daily Respite – Sleep

Everything has to be paid for. Happy, positive emotion creates an energetic debt that will inevitably follow later as negative feelings. And likewise, the energy required to create the apparent separation of the dream environment needs to be balanced, and this daily occurrence is totally accepted as a matter of routine even though questions are still asked today as to what its purpose is...

The mind and body begin to feel sluggish and one loses focus, eventually having no choice but to give up. He loses consciousness, the physical dream evaporates, and he is asleep. There is then a transition period, a middle stage during which short, often seemingly random scenarios can be played out in his mind, some horrifyingly shocking (if our dreamer could remember them), but most may appear to be no more than mundane ramblings. Either way, the vast majority of these dreams are forgotten every night, though they are still an important part of the overall experience of being separate, as the mind is able to work through some issues without it affecting the continuation of the main dream.

Then the main purpose of sleep is achieved, and this is what we refer to as deep, dreamless sleep. This is the opposite polarity to the physical environment, and allows the energetic debt to be repaid as the life experience is temporarily extinguished in the depths of apparent total absence; the energy is replenished from yesterday's imagery, ready for a new day to begin tomorrow. And of course a new day must begin, because the attachment to being separate and to the life that he is living must continue to be satisfied – for now at least.

Karma

With each experience in the world, he is relishing the emotions that arise, or creating them himself through thinking and remembering, if they are not occurring automatically. When something happens to make him unhappy, even after it has physically passed, he will continue to remember and mentally regurgitate the event, over and over, reliving the trauma in a self-imposed hell. Often he claims he'd like it to stop, but suggest to him that he let go of the uncomfortable feeling at the time that it's present and he's likely to immediately jump to the defence of the emotion, declaring he has a RIGHT to feel like this because *that* happened!

And again, this is the secret: The emotion cannot survive when endured consciously. It WILL die, or be made conscious to be more precise (though it will often feel like a death). What our dreamer currently does is feed the emotion further by thinking about the situation, wallowing in the unconscious imaginings, and instead of the emotion being faced and dissolved, it is added to, eventually to withdraw back into the great unconscious. BUT, it will have to re-emerge later in another situation. And THIS is what we call Karma. It really is the past repeating itself.

Death of the Body –
Reincarnation

As if to remind himself subconsciously that this place is temporary and to give him a chance to eventually wake up to his true nature, everything comes to an end. And that includes his own body and present life experience. He sees those around him whom he loves die, though repeatedly fails to grasp the opportunity to make that piece of emotional attachment conscious, and what follows is an extremely painful period of grief during which he's living in the memories of the past. He MAY have learned to distract himself and take his mind off the unhappy thoughts by thinking about something else, and while this is good in that it does not further feed the emotion, it does nothing to dissolve it and make it conscious either. As a result it must still return in another painful situation at a later time, causing more suffering in the 'hope' that the individual will finally reconnect with his being which is behind it all.

Then it comes to one's own death. The dreamer has had his time with this particular dream and it's time to move on. There can initially be an emotionally painful process of saying goodbye and letting go to one's loved ones, if opportunity is provided to do so. But later, as the dream of life and living evaporates, he finds he is connected to a great extent with his own being again, and he knows this is true love. This is what he has longed for, searched for, for so long. This is heaven. He is home again.

But it's not the end. The karmic debt remains from the last life – possibly having accumulated over several lifetimes. The remaining emotion is still in the unconscious and needs to be lived consciously for the cycle to end, so another life must begin. There might be a period of an in-between state, and then he is reborn. And as with a dream when asleep in bed, he has no memory of what's gone before.

Though as we consider what has gone before, we look at what it actually is that is returning. There is God, the one Being behind it all, and there's the emotion that is driving the separation. Occasionally a person claims to have knowledge of a previous life, and it might be true, but if so then it's only a memory of a past dream in which emotion was expressed. The Being itself is the Dreamer, and He's present in every moment, in each and every dream.

So another life begins. And the process continues.

Liberation –
The End of the Cycle

After a number of lifetimes, something happens. Even if one has not tried to be spiritual in any way (in this current life anyway), nevertheless the emotion has been satisfactorily expressed, up to a point at least. And although the emotion has only accidentally been experienced consciously (rather than through a learned method or practice), it's worked, and our dreamer is once again living in the moment. His life is a pleasure. No longer does he seek the next emotional feeling, nor long for those that went before. Whatever occurs does so here and now. Emotional suffering which was previously so frequent in his life is a thing of the past and he feels complete. But also this reuniting with the moment has brought with it the knowledge as to what He is. He knows that everything that is happening is not separate from Him. When describing it He might liken it to the dreams when asleep in bed, or He may use another analogy, or indeed none. The point is that He is 'awake', or Self-aware (in the sense of realising what is often referred to as the Higher Self, rather than the emotional, personal self), or

41

Spiritually Enlightened, or another term which is particularly appropriate, given the nature of this book is God Realised.

As life and living continues, the remaining attachment to being separate is consciously faced and dissolved, and eventually the dream ends. Though, this time there is no need to return in another. There might be a different, finer dream which could occur for a period after this life, if everything is not totally complete and there is still some remaining attachment to being separate, but there is no need for an environment which is capable of providing the circumstances for unhappiness and fear. And this is what is referred to in spiritual teachings of the higher spiritual realms or heavens. The point is that there is no need to return to this environment. And that's what some Eastern teachings describe as ending the cycle of birth and death.

And that would appear to be the end of the story. However, this place, this Being, God, is obviously pretty adept at creating a magnificent dream environment for Itself (you) to experience, full of truly incredible wonders, and it would seem logical to assume it will continue to do so. The idea that having 'woken up' (to His own nature) after a single cycle is complete the dreams will stop forever, does not seem likely. So logic suggests another cycle will begin at a later time (accepting that time only exists, as far as we know anyway, within the dream) and it will happen all over again, eventually.

Why?

(And here we run out of answers.)

We've looked at what happens from before the beginning of the creation and the process that is followed, but why? Why does any of it happen? And perhaps also, who or what is this God we keep talking about (besides my telling you that it's 'you')?

Well, actually, despite the above pages demonstrating unusual knowledge and describing an amazing process, the details of which perhaps the majority of the human race would benefit from knowing, here we run out of answers. It appears that from inside the dream God cannot know His origin. (And we therefore cannot know what the knowledge is outside of the Dream, either, right now, if indeed there is any.) He can know the dream, and Himself as the Dreamer, but he cannot know anything prior to the initial separation.

There are, however, two theories that I am aware of as to why, though neither of these address the question as to where God came from:

1) The most common view is that God is generally complete and needs nothing 'else', beyond Himself; and when any need does arise, He simply creates an environment in which this can be expressed and experienced, after which He returns to his original state. Though, some people go on to describe something called the Akashic Records, which would be a psychic impression in which the knowledge of every experience is recorded.

2) There is another perspective that says at the end of each life cycle, when God is fully realised as Himself, contrary to the above scenario where the cycle ends and God is complete again and nothing has changed, the process has actually been one of literally the conceiving of a new individual, giving birth to it and managing it as it grows to maturity. Thus, rather than God simply having realised Himself in an illusory separation and it ending, a 'new' and separate part of Himself has been 'born' and has grown out of ignorance through right suffering and into an

48

eternally independent and yet forever united (with Him) individual.

I don't know which of the above is correct, but there is something romantic about the latter.

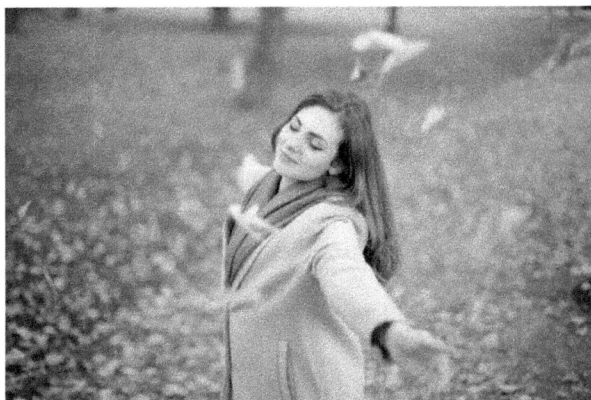

Speeding up the Process

(Part 2)

Right Suffering

In the previous pages we looked at the usual process of indulging in the emotion, thinking about and mentally re-living a situation over and over. And we said this feeds the emotion, making it larger, stronger, and it steadily increases in size on each occasion before withdrawing again to the unconscious where it is stored – until next time. Or, one attempts to avoid the pain, instead thinking about anything else other than the problem until the discomfort has passed. But in both these scenarios the same emotion returns again and again in new situations, offering repeated opportunities to make the energy conscious.

So how do we break the cycle of the same emotion creating painful experiences?

Actually, it's extremely simple, though not easy. It requires a real strength and determination, as the emotion is very strong and persistent, but it can be done.

The practice I'm referring to is simply to remain aware of the moment, of what is happening NOW and not to become lost in the emotion and in unconscious thinking. The urge to think about the problem is likely to be huge, and it's initially extremely difficult to resist as the emotion is very strong. But if you begin by becoming aware of your breathing, this can act as an anchor for the attention as well as calming the mind, and you'll find it's possible to actually watch the emotion rather than being swept away and losing oneself.

The above can take a little practice to get the idea. Though as you'll learn, it doesn't really matter what your attention is on, be it the breathing, other bodily sensations, or even an object you can see in your physical environment, as long as you're aware of observing the emotion. I've picked a physical object at times, whatever I can see in front of me, and just settled my gaze on that until the feelings have gone, all the time aware of the emotion.

As you watch the emotion it can feel like it's squirming, as if you're wrangling a snake, and you're likely to have thoughts running through like "I can't do this! It isn't working!

What's the point? Emotion isn't THAT bad. And anyway, everyone gets unhappy sometimes... Oh look, I've lost it now – I knew that wouldn't work. And now I'm thinking again. So I may as well give up!"

Please don't give up. I know that when one is new to this and doesn't yet have the knowledge and experience of the process that it can seem a bit abstract, but it's an incredible process, and it DOES work. You just have to stick with it and not let the thinking mind and emotions talk you out of it.

The Challenge

The difficulty is twofold:

1) The length of time it will take on each occasion will depend on how much emotional attachment is related to the situation in hand. It might be seconds, minutes, hours or even days. And sometimes it returns in waves, which is helpful as it provides a little respite, but it does dupe one into thinking it's all gone, only to return soon after, and this can lead one to think in the early days that it means you're not doing it right.

2) The feeling each time can be that this discomfort is going to last forever, right up until the instant it evaporates, as if it's trying to put you off and make you give up.

What is likely to happen initially when trying this is you'll 'return to your senses' and to the moment, having been lost in the emotion and in thinking about the problem for quite a while, and will think you can't do it. It's too hard! That's perfectly okay, but don't fall for it. Any time that you spend conscious is energy removed from the emotion. You have no control over at what point you are 'woken up'.

Your job is to hold on to it once you are awake. Over time, as the emotion has been dissolved in various difficult situations, you will find you are being woken up sooner and are able to hold it for longer. But you cannot fail. You can only give up. (Please don't.)

What Happens Next?

Perhaps you're trying this, and having just about reached the point at which you would give up, thinking that this particular unhappy feeling was going to last forever and this entire book was a waste of time, suddenly you notice it's gone. The discomfort, in fact all emotion related to the situation, has gone. Where did it go? When did it go? What happened?

And in its place there might be a feeling of peace, or elation. How amazing is that? And why isn't everyone doing this? Why doesn't everyone know this?

And now, looking again at the situation that was causing the problem, one of three things will have happened:

1) While the emotion has indeed gone, the situation is exactly the same. It just doesn't disturb you anymore;

2) The removal or dissolution of the emotion has revealed a clearer understanding of the problem, and you can see an action that you need to take. Perhaps you had previously

thought there was nothing that you could do, but now you see clearly that there is indeed something and you just HAVE to do it, and everything is fine; or

3) Amazingly, the external situation has changed all by itself. As we've learned in the previous pages, the same energy that is felt as emotion is creating the physical environment, so once the emotion related to it has been made conscious internally, there is no longer any need for the external situation to exist, so it doesn't!

Now THAT'S incredible!

Taking Action

When speaking with people about this process, one of the objections that regularly comes up (likely raised by the emotion in them defending itself) is that one must not avoid the emotions, as if that is what this is about. I trust you see that nothing could be further from the truth. This is about facing it consciously, which is quite the opposite of avoiding it.

However, there is a further vital part of the equation, and that is taking action.

When emotion arises, its nature or impulse as we experience it is to fight to exist, and to continue to do so. It does not want you to remain conscious in the moment, nor to take any action that would help in addressing the situation that has given rise to it. But nevertheless, that is often what is required, and one needs to be very strong to do so. (The emotion itself, of course, knows nothing. It's the effect that it has on the thinking process that I'm really referring to when I talk about what the emotion 'wants'.)

Whilst mentally holding on to the emotion, watching it and yet separate from it, there is also a knowledge of what it relates to. This is integral to the emotion and means you don't have to try to remember why you are unhappy or disturbed. You KNOW exactly why you feel like that.

So, as you are observing the emotion and feeling the urge to get lost in the thinking process but resisting it, look intelligently at the situation itself. Don't think ABOUT the problem, look AT it (remaining aware of your physical surroundings, so you don't get sucked into the imagination). Of course, there are some situations where there is never going to be anything you can do, physically anyway. But as well as taking action, one's understanding of a problem can change. Without the emotion clouding one's perspective, a whole fresh outlook can develop – of all things, actually, but particularly the situation at hand – and life generally begins to improve.

With regards to taking action, the trick is to be PREPARED to take the action. The action itself is not the point. Addressing the emotion is the point, and doing what is required so that one can return to a peaceful state of existence within. There will be times when you see an action that you feel you must take, but right now it's not possible to do so (maybe it's the middle of the night, for example). And then when the time comes, you find there really is no need to take it. What was actually required was for you to be prepared to take the action, genuinely. And that was enough. This process is very fluid and can change enormously moment to moment.

In summary, one observes the emotion when it arises, remaining open to taking action as necessary and watching out for any changes in the situation. But don't lose sight of the fact that it's the emotion that is the point, not the action.

Moods and Anxiety

Because we can have so much emotion in us, there can be times when it spills over and for no apparent reason one wakes up in a bad mood. So how does one deal with that?

Actually, it's even easier – or rather, simpler – than dealing with a specific problem, because there is not the distraction of an actual situation to contend with. It's just emotion with attachment to nothing but itself.

So just observe it, as we've learned so far. Connect with the breathing, or something else, and watch. And as we've said, emotion cannot survive with the attention on it. It needs the attention to be lost in thoughts and thinking, and not acting like a spotlight on itself. So by watching the mood, you'll find it will soon dissolve.

And the same is the case with anxiety. Any emotion only has a relatively short lifespan when being directly observed. Anxiety tends to revolve around a thought process. So, stilling the mind, connecting within and watching the feeling are generally enough to switch off the anxiety, as long as you can stay aware. But do remember the rest of the process with regards to looking at the situation (again, not thinking ABOUT it) and watching out for any action that could help, because anxiety or not, sometimes the problem can be addressed by taking physical action, or by seeing the situation differently. (In other words, don't assume because you suffer from anxiety that there is automatically nothing you can do.)

Stillness is IT

So what are we looking for ultimately? What is there when the emotion is not present?

Well, have a look now. Take a breath and feel your bodily sensations, and see what is inside. Is there anything there? Or is it peaceful, or warm, or stillness, or nothing? Any and all of these could be used to describe what one might feel there, as well as words like 'complete', 'whole' and even 'love'. And of course it is love, true love. This is what love feels like when it's not filled with emotion. And yet THAT is why it's also so hard to keep hold of this. There is little or no feeling there.

And this is important to acknowledge, because having spent one's entire life to date experiencing everything through the imaginary world of thinking and worrying, and enjoying the frequent highs and often painful lows that accompanied it, when one finally connects with one's own being and finds there is nothing here, the mind thinks it's doing it wrong: 'This can't be it!'

But of course it is it. One can only feel what one is not — what one is separate from. Whilst admittedly everything is one, emotions are unconscious energy and therefore the conscious mind can experience them. This is why we need the dream of separation. No separation equals no experience.

So when you are aware of being aware, and find there is no feeling there, please do not think you've lost it. It means you're doing it perfectly. It's just that at this moment there is no emotion that needs to be experienced. So stick with it. As you spend more time in this space, it gradually deepens and the quality becomes quite magnificent; but also, the knowledge as to who and what you are, and that this place is all 'you', is made available. So keep going.

Speeding up the Attention

When you start doing this, it's likely that several minutes or even hours following an emotional experience (depending on how disturbing it was) you'll suddenly catch yourself thinking, and you'll see that you've been lost in unconscious thinking ever since the event happened. But don't worry at all, for if you do, you'll have fallen into the trap of thinking and worrying about thinking and worrying, and you'll be lost again. Instead, just start now: feel the breathing and watch what is there, and look intelligently at the situation as we've said. And keep doing it.

After several times of doing this, you'll find you begin to get there quicker. Whatever it is that brings you back to the moment is beginning to do so earlier as your attention speeds up. And you can begin to dissolve the emotion sooner. It's not long before it's no longer hours before you begin to face and dissolve the emotion from a difficult situation, but one hour, or thirty minutes, or ten minutes. And as time passes and you continue to practise this, the emotion in the unconscious is steadily reducing and growing weaker, and your conscious mind is getting stronger and quicker, and you are growing in self-knowledge and self-awareness.

******

By way of a personal example, for me now, I can have a thought about a situation that MIGHT happen but has not yet materialised. And immediately my attention is there, simply looking at the subtle urge to think about it, imagine it, and I am aware that the, albeit relatively mild emotional energy that brought the thought to the surface is exposed even though there isn't actually a feeling yet. And then, sometimes as quickly as that, it's gone. But more importantly the situation never has to materialise physically, as I've removed the energy from it before it even happens. I've already 'learned the lesson' (made the emotion conscious, or released that piece of karma), so there is nothing left to create the difficulty.

Another common situation for me now is that I might be waiting for something or to hear back from someone, and I catch myself

84

thinking about this and am immediately aware that there is attachment there. Again, it's not a feeling; it's too subtle for that now. It's just an urge to let go of the moment and mentally look forward to the next. And instantly the knowledge is present that THIS is why the reply (for example) has not materialised yet. My attachment to the situation is holding the reply away, suspending the circumstances exactly as they are and extending the period so the emotion may experience itself. And as usual, as soon as I see this I drop it, connect with the stillness or sense of 'I am' (or the breathing, etc.) and resist the suddenly extremely weak impulse to go into the imagination again. (Just seeing it is enough to remove so much of its energy, and it can't survive long as I look at it.)

It's also not unusual for the situation to change, as is the way. Once I've recognised the attachment to receiving the reply and have dealt with this, something else may happen, or I notice I have benefitted in some way from the delay, be it that I remember something or hear something else related to it, or I suddenly see that there's something that I need to do first. There are the sayings 'everything happens for a reason' and 'everything is connected', and these are of course the case.

And having said the above, there's still no guarantee the reply will ever arrive. It usually will, quite quickly once the emotion has gone. But the delay or absence could also be part of a larger lesson, and while that little piece of emotion has gone, there is still emotion connected to the situation as a whole, and this will be exposed as time progresses.

(The above description is far removed from my being lost in unconscious thinking and wallowing in emotion for several hours following each and every disturbing situation, as was the case when I started doing this, so it shows what can happen if one perseveres. It does get easier, and life and living get better. But it starts with not accepting unhappiness within oneself, and mustering both the courage and the strength to face it consciously and take action as necessary, each and every time.)

What About Happy Thoughts?

Yeah, what about happy thoughts? We've been having a go at negative emotion, but what about happy feelings, and thinking about good times? That's okay isn't it?

Actually, I said earlier that the pendulum of emotion swings both ways, and as such, happy thinking is the flip side of unhappy thinking; one cannot have one without the other. If you enjoy thinking about happy things, remembering nice thoughts and imagining better times, when later faced with a real-life situation that is emotionally uncomfortable, you will find you won't be able to stop thinking about it. The emotion has been strengthened by feeding it when thinking previously, albeit positively, so it will take control when things turn negative. So as difficult as it is, one needs to do what one can to remain aware now, whatever one is doing, and either watch the emotion if it's there or remain in the stillness of being aware if there is no emotion there. The point, as ever, is to remain aware and separate from the mind and emotion.

And this is perhaps the issue generally for everyone who is new to this. As I described at the beginning of this book, God (i.e. you) loves the emotional ups and downs. He relishes in the drama and excitement and really does not want it to stop. And if you find you are happy leaving things as they are, as difficult as they might be, that's okay. No judgement from me. The important thing is that you know what is happening and why.

However, do not take this to mean there can be no enjoyment of life. Quite to the contrary – one can enjoy EVERYTHING. The point is that one is aware of oneself and enjoys whatever happens consciously, rather than being lost in the imagination and experiencing things unconsciously. And in such a state living can become effortless and a real pleasure, but it's certainly not the cold unfeeling state that the emotional thinking mind would imagine it to be.

Have You Suffered Enough?

This is the question really, because no-one is going to fight to remain aware and conscious in the midst of an emotionally painful situation, even knowing everything in this book, if they don't have a very good reason for doing so. And perhaps the most likely reason will be that they have had enough pain, enough unhappiness, and cannot accept it any longer.

Though, this is not as common as it might sound, and although everyone has suffered heartache and painful losses during their life, some possibly too horrific for another to contemplate, it still might not be enough for the individual to even want to try to resist the incredible momentum of the emotion, and deny the urge to go off into the world of imagination, thinking and worrying. And as a result, the emotion will have to continue to repeat itself in the circumstances of their life.

(I guess if the need to realise the truth, or 'God', and to reconnect with one's true nature was strong enough, then that might be enough. But the effort required in denying the drive of the emotion to go into the imagination can be immense, so the need itself would have to be strong enough to at least equal that.)

All-day Awareness

The practice is all day, every day, whenever one remembers, to connect with the sense of 'I am' and the knowledge that I exist (and ideally not just when one is faced with an emotionally difficult situation), and to become the observer of what *is* rather than an unconscious passenger. Sure, it takes effort. But as I said earlier, there is absolutely no failure. One cannot do it wrong. One can only stop doing it. If the intention is present and the wish to 'wake up' established, then life will keep waking you up, bringing you back to the moment. Then it's up to you whether you hold on to it as long as you can, or immediately let go and return to the relative stupor of the unconscious living. (As we've said, this really is YOUR life. The emotion will have to be made conscious ONE day, but it needn't be today!)

Each time you attempt to remain conscious, watching, regardless of how long you are able to remain there, even if it's only moments, the work has been done and the next time it will wake you up that little bit sooner and you will be able to hold it that little bit longer. Just keep doing it.

The Never-ending Story

Sometimes it can feel like it really is never-ending. The emotion and the difficult situations just keep on coming one after another, and it seems endless. Even once one has connected enough within oneself to have the knowledge that 'this is all me and I'm creating this (unconsciously)', the emotion must keep being stirred nonetheless. There will be times when all seems good and you might think you're through it, but it cannot remain in the unconscious indefinitely. If you have not realised your true self yet, become God Realised and in constant and conscious union with everything, then there is more to come and it has to be exposed so as to be made conscious. So the emotion WILL keep coming and difficult times will continue to happen, whilst there is sufficient emotion there.

Actually, whilst one has a body, there is still some attachment present to some extent which is keeping the dream going, so one has never totally finished. Though, thankfully, the emotional suffering ends quite a while prior to the dream ending.

Living in the Moment

So here we are, back at the beginning —
almost.

Enough of the emotion has now been faced
and made conscious, and the person is living
in the moment as a result, liberated from
emotional suffering, and each moment of life
is a pleasure. Not exciting as such, without
the emotional ups and downs, but certainly
enjoyable.

And it *had* been the attachment to
experiencing 'more' that was forever in the
background, hidden from view in the
unconscious mind but not dormant and
always 'pushing' from beneath the surface,
that was responsible for the incessant
thinking, imagining and worrying. But that's
gone now too. There's just 'being' again,
aware and watching: God is awake, albeit still
dreaming, but aware that this is His dream
and what exists is because of the remaining
attachment within Him that is continuing to
create what is required.

So life continues, though not quite as before.
Everything seems simpler, easier and

effortless. Situations can still happen, but the resulting emotion is slight and rapidly dissolved, and the physical situation passes quickly and painlessly.

So this is the Heaven on Earth that He knew was possible. This is His Garden of Eden that He abandoned so long ago when He lost his innocence, when He lost His connection with His true nature and forgot who He was. Now He's home again.

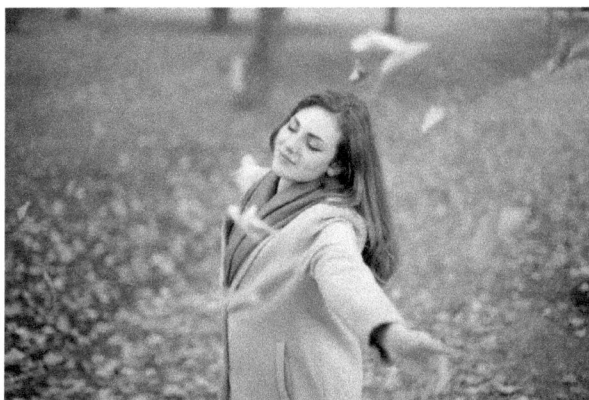

It Works – Thank You

In case you needed a little more motivation, here are a few words from others who have tried this:

"This is a massive revelation for me. I went to therapy for months and got nothing as useful and practical out of it as this. I woke up positive and relieved today having watched a load of your videos last night where this method was explained in various ways. The idea of reclaiming the emotional energy makes sense, and if we are creating this reality out of this energy then presumably my life experience should vastly increase as the newly claimed energy is channelled towards the creation of now rather than reconstructing the past. Shame I didn't hear this 25 years ago, but maybe I needed to accumulate enough pain to galvanise and make the effort to stop the momentum of the juggernaut in order to dissolve this, bit by bit." – YouTube subscriber

"Yes Nick, it can be uncomfortable, but it's bearable... trust in the process does the job. Thank you" – YouTube subscriber

"You're amazing Nick and I'm truly glad and happy that you're in my dream to guide to me. One day I'll be able to share all this wisdom with my son and guide him with his life. You have brought up a warm and enlightened sensation in me!! I like the way you do that! Thanks again" – Facebook visitor

"I just watched your Master in the Mirror video. Sweet Jesus, thank you Nick. God Bless you. God Bless you x's infinity. There is feeling of connection happening. I have been so confused going through this nightmare of trying to reconnect on my 'own' and from just that one video of yours there is a deeper Stillness and deeper sense of Self. I could cry. Absolutely have tears. Thank you from the bottom of my heart." – Facebook visitor

"From your meetings I have realised what I really want in life - it's the peace. I'm fed up of my anxieties and everyday emotional rollercoaster. I need to be at the stillness and attract a relationship around that. I'm also going to therapy less and less now. I know

there's not much need, thanks to you."
– Meeting attendee

"It's so clear to me now. It's all about the emotion. Why doesn't everyone know this?"
– Reader of autobiography

Final Word from Nick Roach

Thank you for reading this book, and I hope you have enjoyed it.

I also hope you can sense that it's far more than just a story and you'll be able to make use of what is here. Try the method a few times and you'll be amazed at how effective it is and you too will wonder why everyone doesn't know this.

If you would like to know more, as well as the three books mentioned at the beginning, we have a large website and from there we have links to our YouTube channel with over forty videos, and our Facebook page. We also have a Facebook group, for anyone who would like to discuss this with others.

If you would like to contact me, please feel free to do so and I'll do my best to help.

Nick Roach

Other Publications

Enlightenment, The Simple Path

Essays in Truth – Glimpses into Reality

A Dream It May Be, but the Dream Goes On!

Website: www.nickroach.uk

www.ingramcontent.com/pod-product-compliance
Lightning Source LLC
Chambersburg PA
CBHW060511030426
42337CB00015B/1853